Following in Darwin's footsteps

By Aileen O'Riordan and Pat Triggs

Featuring fun activities inspired by Darwin and introduced
by Lily, Ash and Joseph from www.greatplanthunt.org

Developed by RBG Kew, commissioned and funded by The Wellcome Trust

 wellcometrust

Kew
PLANTS PEOPLE
POSSIBILITIES

 DARWIN200

Chapter 1: Introduction
Charles Darwin, 1809-1882

The next time you see a ten pound note, turn it over and take a closer look at the picture on the back. The Victorian gentleman with the bushy eyebrows and long, white beard is Charles Darwin. The ship sailing into the distance is HMS Beagle. When he was in his twenties Darwin sailed around the world on the Beagle and the experiences he had then helped to make him one of Britain's finest scientists. Those experiences also led him to a new way of thinking that people are still talking about 200 years after he was born. Darwin's most famous book explained his daring new idea and was called *On the Origin of Species*. When it was published in 1859, every single copy was snapped up on the first day. (You can read all about his ground-breaking new idea, evolution by natural selection, in chapter 8).

But having an amazing big idea was only part of it. In 1864 Darwin was awarded the Copley medal by the Royal Society. That's a bit like an athlete winning an Olympic gold medal, or maybe gold medals in several Olympic Games. Darwin won his medal for his many achievements as a biologist and naturalist.

So what was it about Darwin that made him so special?

Darwin studied and wrote about a wide range of topics. His first book to be published was all about rocks and his last was about the life and work of worms. In between he wrote about how coral reefs are made, how climbing plants move and the mysterious life of insect-eating plants. Throughout his life Darwin wanted passionately to understand or explain what he saw. He really noticed things and thought about them. He never stopped asking questions. Darwin also developed very methodical ways

> Darwin always remembered the exact moment of his big idea: "I can remember the very spot in the road... The solution, as I believe, is that the modified offspring of all dominant and increasing forms tend to become adapted to many and highly diversified places in the economy of nature." [1]

to record information and investigate mysteries so he could find answers. Most importantly he recorded details about an enormous number of different things he saw in many different places, followed the evidence and was brave enough to come up with ideas that seemed logical — even if they were almost unthinkable.

In many ways, though, Darwin was quite ordinary. He didn't do very well at school and used to get into trouble with his dad and his teachers. As a grown man he was nervous about speaking in front of a crowd of people. Instead he preferred to stay home with his wife, family and his books. He was a great collector, experimenter and thinker. Even before he started school, he loved to scoop up and take home anything that grew, flew or crawled.

Darwin was also quite lucky. He made many friends because of his openness, his curiosity and his enthusiasm for natural history. One of them, John Henslow, a Professor of Botany, recommended him as naturalist and captain's companion on board HMS Beagle, a navy ship ordered to South America to survey and map the coastline. Aged 22, Darwin's dream of seeing nature in the tropics came true. As the ship's naturalist it was his job to study the plants, rocks and animals that he found along the way. He also read a lot and wrote about the things he saw, from amazing blood-sucking bats and climbing plants, to puzzling fossils and erupting volcanoes.

Darwin was a very curious boy. In 1938 he remembered, "I distinctly recollect the desire… to be able to know something about every pebble in front of the hall door." [2]

During the five-year journey he collected, recorded and sent home hundreds of specimens. When he arrived back in Britain in 1836, Darwin found he was famous. His notebooks, diaries and letters recording the journey were the basis for travel books and scientific enquiries. He said that the voyage of the Beagle was the most important event in his life.

After his amazing voyage, Darwin got married and settled down in Kent at Down House. One of the first things he did was to build a sand-covered path around the house. The path wound through the woods and returned to the house along the side of a hedge-lined field. Every day Darwin and his dog would take a 'thinking walk' along this path.

He used this time to clear his head, think about his experiments and to watch the local wildlife through the seasons. Darwin did most of his work at home in his study-cum-workroom. His children often played or drew while he worked and sometimes he got them to help him. Some scientists thought his ideas about the origin of species and natural selection were wrong, but he also had many supporters. Many well-known scientists of the time were visitors at Down House. Special friends like Joseph Hooker, who became the Director of the Royal Botanic Gardens at Kew, visited to work and talk.

Darwin had excellent spotting skills – and he knew it! He said to his son Francis, "I think that I am superior to the common run of men in noticing things which easily escape attention, and in observing them carefully." [3]

People loved chatting to Darwin. His friend Lubbock said, "An hour with him... proved a wonderful cordial and brushed away the cobwebs of the imagination like a breath of fresh air." [4]

Darwin was a great believer in writing things down, from detailed observations to half-formed ideas. He scribbled, drew pictures and diagrams. His notes show that he didn't always understand what he saw at first. If he got stuck on a problem he would do an experiment or ask one of his fellow experts, friends or even a total stranger for help. They nearly always gave it. Perhaps that's because Darwin was a kind, patient and polite person. He always remembered to thank people for their help — particularly the plant, animal and fossil experts who became his friends — and he didn't like to show off.

When Darwin died, it was these friends who organised for him to be buried at Westminster Abbey. His gravestone sits nears others belonging to kings and queens as well as some of our country's other great thinkers, writers, musicians and scientists.

Challenge questions

- What do you think makes someone amazing?
- Does someone need to be famous to be great?
- Can you think of any ideas that are brave and unusual? How would you like people to describe you — smart, fast, funny or kind?
- Darwin thought he was particularly good at noticing things — what do you think you are good at?

Get sticky

Throughout his life Charles Darwin collected anything that grew, crept or flew. He would often take a walk to collect samples or think his ideas through. Why not take your own 'Thinking Walk'?

Take some masking tape or sticky tape. Wrap it around your wrist, sticky side up. Get a friend to help and remember not to make it too tight.

Take a 'Thinking Walk' outdoors and pick up small bits and bobs. Petals, seeds and small leaves work well.

Carefully cut off your nature wristband and keep it safe.

Do the same again in different seasons to see the difference!

Chapter 2:
Darwin the Lookout

Darwin didn't always behave as others wanted him to, but was the first to admit it! As he told his son Francis, "I was in many ways, a naughty boy." 1

1817–1831

* Shrewsbury, Edinburgh and Cambridge
* Darwin aged 8-22

It was four o'clock. School was over and Charles Robert Darwin was busy. He was lying in the grass with his chin propped in his hands doing one of the things he liked best. What was he doing? He was looking hard at what was happening just past the end of his nose.

He was looking at the insects buzzing among the flowers, he was watching the worms moving in the damp earth, he was noticing how the plants grew. But he wasn't just looking, he was also thinking and wondering. Why did the insects go to one flower more than another? Why were the leaves of that plant so different from the one next to it? What were the worms doing to the earth? In fact he was thinking so hard that he didn't hear his three big sisters calling, "Bobby, Bobby, where are you? It's time for tea."

They were running around the garden of the big house where they all lived, fussing as usual. They didn't know, and neither did he, that the eight-year-old boy they called Bobby, who was late for tea, would grow up to be the famous scientist, Charles Darwin.

Caroline found him. "There you are," she said. "You should have been back from school ages ago. And you're covered in mud." Charles got up. He was tall for his age with grey-blue eyes and dark brown hair. "And what have you got in your pockets today?" asked Caroline. Charles put his hand into his bulging pocket and pulled out shells, stones, coins and leaves. Caroline wasn't surprised. She knew that Charles was as crazy about collecting things as he was about looking at insects, plants, rocks and animals. He was always wondering why they were like they were and why they did what they did. Caroline knew that Charles really only liked doing what he was interested in; and what he was interested in was being outside, going for long walks, exploring the countryside and fishing in the River Severn, which ran past their garden. He could also be quite naughty, scrumping apples and making up wild stories.

Back at the house tea was ready. Erasmus ('Ras for short) Charles' older brother was wondering why the girls were making a fuss. "You know what he's like. He's always dreaming. Remember the time he was walking on the old city walls, thinking about something or other, and he managed to fall off. He survived. He always does."

A year later when Charles was nine he went, like 'Ras, to Shrewsbury School for boys. It was a boarding school but so near their house that the boys could run home, and often did. Charles was not a star pupil. He just wasn't interested in things like Latin and Greek that people nearly two hundred years ago thought boys should know. When he was 13 he and 'Ras set up a science lab in the garden shed at home; that was much more exciting. The two brothers were often there late into the night experimenting with potions and powders and

making smelly things. Their sisters thought they might blow up the house. As a grown-up, Charles said he had learned a lot from that science lab about how to do science experiments. At the time, Charles' father, Dr Robert Darwin, was not impressed. "You will be a disgrace to yourself and your family," he told Charles.

When Charles was 16 he was sent to Edinburgh to study to be a doctor like his father, grandfather and brother. But he knew it was not for him. For one thing he couldn't bear to see all the blood during operations. Instead he joined a club to study nature. He read a lot of books about rocks and learned to stuff animals and birds, which was very fashionable at the time. Charles also became a bird-watcher and filled his notebooks with details about what he saw. He also went hunting and shooting, which he found very exciting.

As a child, Darwin loved to spot and collect things. He said, "By the time I went to school my taste for natural history and collecting was well developed. I tried to make out the names of plants and collected all sorts of things, shells, seals, franks, coins, and minerals." [2]

Going on a tropical adventure to see more of the natural world was something Darwin had always dreamed of. In fact he couldn't stop thinking about it, and said, "My head is running around the Tropics... My enthusiasm is so great that I cannot hardly sit still." 3

All these things turned out to be very useful later when Charles went on his scientific adventures. But his father was afraid his son was becoming someone who was

Darwin's dad did not approve of him spending all his time as a naturalist. "You will be a disgrace to yourself and your family," he told his son. 4

only interested in "shooting, dogs, and rat catching." So he sent Charles to Cambridge University with a plan that he would become a country vicar.

But Charles just became more and more interested in learning about the plants and creatures around him. He was still collecting things; this time it was beetles that fascinated him. At Cambridge he found lots of friends and teachers to learn from and encourage him, especially Professor Henslow, who said he never stopped asking questions. Charles passed his examinations but what he really wanted to do was pack his bags and go on a tropical adventure to see nature in other countries. He would have to wait a while for that. But his chance would come.

Challenge questions

- Can you spot insects and flowers in the grass?
- What grows around your house?
- What are you good at spotting? Do you know all the makes of fast cars or the names of different breeds of dogs? Or maybe you are good at recognising faces?
- What do you like doing that might help to make you a scientist?

Watch out, trees about!

As a young boy, Charles Darwin was very fond of a sweet chestnut tree in his garden. He and his sister had their own special seats in it.

At different times of year you can smell its flowers or leaves, plant its seeds or photograph it in the snow.

Find a tree near home and make it your own. Make regular visits to see how it is getting on.

Before you know it you'll be giving it a name!

Get to know it well by making bark rubbings with crayons and paper. Tree trunks change in width at different times during the day – can you measure the trunk and spot the difference?

Remember:
- Never wander off alone.
- Make sure a grown up knows where you are
- Climbing trees can be dangerous. Leave it to the squirrels unless an adult is helping out.

If you wait quietly, animals and insects that use your tree for food or shelter might come out.

Chapter 3: Darwin the Discoverer

> Darwin knew that his long journey had changed his life. He said, "The voyage of the Beagle has been by far the most important event in my life, and has determined my whole career." 1

1831–36

❀ Voyage of the Beagle
❀ Darwin aged 22-27

HMS Beagle was sailing out of Plymouth on its way to South America to make maps of the coastline. On board, Charles Darwin looked round the cabin where he would be living for the next five years. It was VERY small. What's more there was a large table in the middle and one of the ship's masts came up through the floor. Darwin would have to sling his hammock over the table and sleep with his nose almost against the ceiling.

It was two days after Christmas and Darwin had been away from home for weeks. How was he feeling? A bit sad to be leaving all the people he loved most, and a little afraid because he didn't know what was going to happen. But most of all, he felt excited and lucky to be on this ship, going to places he had dreamed about since he was a little boy. Darwin smiled as he remembered the book he had borrowed from a friend at school. It was called 'The Wonders of the World' and he had read it again and again, longing to travel the world to find out about places, people and things he had never seen.

But Darwin being on board the Beagle might never have happened. He had left Cambridge University and was expecting to spend the rest of his life as a vicar in a country church. This was a job which would give him plenty of time to go on collecting, observing and investigating rocks, plants, birds and everything to do with natural history, which was his passion. Then John Henslow, his friend and teacher from Cambridge, wrote to Darwin. He said that Robert FitzRoy, the captain of HMS Beagle, was looking for someone to keep him company on the voyage, and also to be the ship's naturalist. That person would have to explore, collect and record specimens of rocks, plants, and animals. Darwin knew this was his dream job. He managed to persuade his father to let him go and to pay for everything needed. Luckily, Darwin's father was a rich and generous man.

The first few weeks at sea were not easy. Darwin was very seasick and it took him a while to work out how to get in and out of his hammock. But he didn't regret being on board or stop feeling excited. He got on well with the two other young men who shared his tiny cabin, and with FitzRoy, who was quite grumpy. He had all the equipment he had brought — pistols, rifle, telescope, compass, microscope, notebooks, collecting jars — safely stowed; he had his precious books on a shelf. In fact he had everything a scientific explorer needed. Soon he was writing to his sister Caroline that the two metre by two metre space he had to work in was particularly 'comfortable for all sorts of work, everything is close to hand.'

The Beagle spent four years along the coast of South America, going round Cape Horn and up to the Galápagos Islands. Then they sailed across the Pacific to New Zealand, Australia, the Cocos Islands and, returning home, stopped at South Africa.

Wherever the ship stopped Darwin went exploring. He couldn't wait to be off the ship and to be outdoors 'with the sky for a roof and the ground for a table.' And everything he saw amazed, delighted and intrigued him. In Cambridge he had been obsessed

For Darwin, discovering unrecorded plant and animal life was glorious. In Bahia, Darwin once said, "I returned to the shore, treading on volcanic rocks, hearing the notes of unknown birds, and seeing new insects fluttering about still newer flowers. It has been... a glorious day." [2]

with collecting beetles. In Brazil he was in 'a delirium of delight' because 'whichever way a beetle-hunter looks fresh treasures meet his eyes.' Of another glorious day he wrote, 'I returned to the shore, treading on volcanic rocks, hearing the notes of unknown birds and seeing new insects fluttering about still newer flowers... It was like giving a blind man eyes.'

Darwin kept a diary where he described 'carefully and vividly all that I had seen.' He saw a lot and met many different people. He went up rivers, climbed mountains, crossed deserts and hunted on horseback with South American cowboys. He saw volcanoes and felt earthquakes. He discovered fossil remains of giant extinct animals, watched icebergs

Darwin was amazed by the plant and animal life he saw in the Galapagos islands. In 1835 he said, "The natural history of this archipelago is very remarkable: it seems to be a little world within itself; the greater number of its inhabitants, both vegetable and animal, being found nowhere else." 3

crumble and crash into the sea and discovered more amazing plants than he ever thought possible.

Wherever he went, he collected specimens. Darwin packed and bottled bones, rocks, animal skins and bird feathers. He carefully pressed hundreds of plants. He was careful to write down exactly where he found a plant growing or an insect living; he described their parts and sometimes drew rough pictures. Darwin looked carefully and noticed when things were different.

Whenever he could Darwin sent home what he had collected with some of his notebooks and diaries. And he was always writing letters.

When he got back he found he was quite famous and considered a 'scientist'. The things he found and noticed on his travels stayed with him and kept him asking questions for the rest of his life. Why do some things look alike and some so different? Why are things different in places where the climate is the same?

The young man who felt sad, afraid and excited as the Beagle started on its voyage didn't know that this journey was going to be the most important event in his life. Nor did he know that his questions and careful investigations would lead him to a very big idea indeed, one of the biggest and most important in all science.

Challenge questions

- What have you seen that made you curious, made you ask questions?
- How do you feel when you see or smell or touch growing things?
- Have you ever stood under a tree in the rain? What did you notice?
- What do you think is the most useful plant we have?

Bed bugs

While Charles Darwin was in Brazil he spotted amazing clicking butterflies, jumping spiders, flesh-eating beetles and armies of ants. What creepy-crawlies live in your neighbourhood?

Did you ask the owner if you can borrow it?

Look here!

Find an old white sheet and place it under the branches of a bush or tree. Don't forget to tell a grown-up where you are going. Also, take someone else with you - it's more fun with a friend.

Gently shake the branches and see if any bugs fall onto the sheet. Before they scuttle off, take a good look.

Look for these clues

 • Nibbled leaves?

 • Tunnels burrowed in the bark or leaves?

 • Webs between leaves or silken blankets wrapped around spiders' eggs?

 • Other eggs lurking under the leaves?

Gently shake the sheet so that the bugs can find their way home.

Get all the bugs out before you give the sheet back!

Look at your chosen shrub or tree. To you it's a plant, but to the mini-beasts that live there it's a cafe, family home or hotel. What were your bugs up to before you came along?

Chapter 4: Darwin the Thinker

During the Beagle voyage, Darwin loved arriving at exotic destinations. As he once said, "The… peculiar atmosphere of the tropics was one of great interest: if indeed a person fresh from sea and walking for the first time in a grove of Cocoa-nut trees, can be a judge of anything but his own happiness." [1]

1831–36

❀ Voyage of the Beagle
❀ Darwin aged 22–27

Two days after Christmas in 1831 Charles Darwin stood on the deck of HMS Beagle as it left Plymouth to sail round the world. What happened on that voyage turned him from an ordinary person into a scientist.

What was Darwin doing on the Beagle? He was the naturalist. Wherever the ship stopped he had to find things like plants, animals, birds, rocks and fossils. It was his dream job. He got it because he was an enthusiastic collector, was very interested in the natural world and he knew a bit about rocks. He wasn't particularly clever at school, but he was good at noticing things and thinking about what he saw.

On the voyage Darwin kept a detailed diary. He sent back samples of the things he collected. He wrote letters about what he was seeing. He read books which gave him more ideas and made him look more carefully and ask more questions. He was always thinking and coming up with new ideas about the things he saw.

Darwin was often seasick and sometimes ill with fever. He would lie in his hammock, which was strung from the ceiling of his tiny cabin, look through the little window above him at the sky outside and wish the ship would arrive in some port where he could get off and go exploring. When it did, his thoughts were all about how being on land and walking among all the tropical plants made him feel. He had read about the plants in books, and dreamed about seeing them but actually being among them took his breath away. Fresh from the sea and walking for the first time in a grove of coconut palms, Darwin had never felt so happy. He thought the amazing colours and shapes of the flowers would make a florist go wild. In the forest he looked up at the thick foliage and then down at his feet and found he was walking on the beautiful and elegant leaves of hundreds of different kinds of ferns and mimosas. He could hardly think of words to describe how he felt; he was so full of wonder and astonishment.

Travelling inland, Darwin did another kind of thinking. He gathered information from local people about plants and how they used them. In one place the forest had been cleared so beans, sugar cane and rice could be planted. Darwin was interested in what people told him about a plant where every part was useful. The leaves and stalks were eaten by the horses, the roots were ground into a pulp which, when pressed dry and baked, became the basic floury substance that everyone ate. But he also heard that the juice of the very same plant was highly poisonous and a few years before a cow had died from drinking it. That fact intrigued Darwin and made him thoughtful.

Even being caught in a tropical storm made Darwin think. He was sheltering under a tree with leaves and branches that were so thick that English rain would never get though them. In a couple of minutes a little

Another big inspiration was the variety of plants. According to Darwin, he was "attracted by the extreme elegance of the leaves of numberless species of Ferns & Mimosas… wonder, astonishment and sublime devotion fill and elevate the mind." [2]

torrent of water was flowing down the trunk. That would explain, thought Darwin, why everything was so green underfoot there and so brown at home. A gentle English shower would have evaporated before it hit the ground.

There was one thing on his travels that angered Darwin. He couldn't understand why so many of the people in the places he visited in South America were slaves. The owners of the slaves gave him many explanations about why it was necessary and not wrong to have slaves and make them work the land. But Darwin thought they were wrong and their arguments were weak.

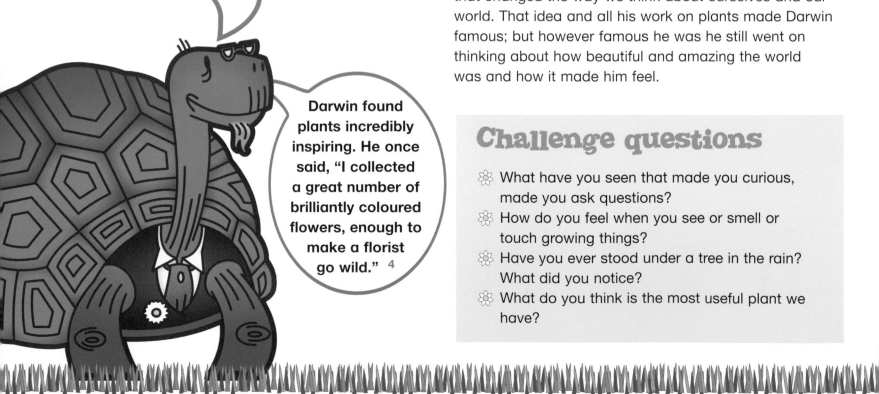

The climates in places Darwin travelled to were different to the ones he knew from home. He saw plants that were well adapted to their environment. In the Brazilian rainforest he got caught in a tropical storm and said, "I tried to find shelter under a tree so thick that it would never have been penetrated by common English rain, yet here… a little torrent flowed down the trunk. …If the showers were like those of a colder clime, the moisture would be absorbed or evaporated before reaching the ground." 3

Darwin found plants incredibly inspiring. He once said, "I collected a great number of brilliantly coloured flowers, enough to make a florist go wild." 4

Darwin thought that being the naturalist on the Beagle was the most important thing that happened to him in his life. When he got back to Britain he went on thinking about all the things he had seen and collected, working with all the careful notes he had made. He went on being curious and asking questions. He experimented, turned ideas and tricky problems over and over in his head. Sometimes he needed to work alone. But when he got stuck or needed help he turned to friends and fellow scientists for added brain power.

One of the results of his thinking was a really big idea that changed the way we think about ourselves and our world. That idea and all his work on plants made Darwin famous; but however famous he was he still went on thinking about how beautiful and amazing the world was and how it made him feel.

Challenge questions

- What have you seen that made you curious, made you ask questions?
- How do you feel when you see or smell or touch growing things?
- Have you ever stood under a tree in the rain? What did you notice?
- What do you think is the most useful plant we have?

From handy herbs to useful yuccas

What happened this morning? Did you get dressed, wash your face with soap, eat a bowl of cereal and clean your teeth?
You might be surprised to find that we rely on plants a lot. They are all around us!

While travelling in Tahiti, Darwin slept in a shelter made by local people. He woke up early one morning to the sound of heavy rain pounding on his banana leaf roof. In his travel journal he wrote about the people he met and how they used plants in their everyday lives. What do you use plants for?

Plants for making things

Plants for shelter

Plants for medicine, health and wellbeing

Plants for food

Plants for inspiring

I'm going to make a collage

That's a good idea. Look through these old magazines and cut out good pictures for it

Chapter 5: Darwin the Collector

Darwin was very proud about being recognized as a proper collector. He said, "No poet ever felt more delight at seeing his first poem published than I did at seeing in Stephen's Illustrations of British Insects the magic words, 'captured by C. Darwin, Esq'". [1]

1828–1836

* Cambridge and the voyage of the Beagle
* Darwin aged 19-27

It was 1828 and at Cambridge University there was a new craze — beetle frenzy. Charles Darwin was in a desperate contest with another student to have the best collection of unusual beetles. Out beetle hunting one afternoon, Darwin carefully peeled back the bark of a tree. Amazing! There were two rare beetles. He caught them, one in each hand.

"Beetles Babington won't have these," he thought triumphantly. Then, out of the corner of his eye Darwin spotted another beetle, equally unusual. What to do? He couldn't bear to lose another specimen. Darwin quickly popped one of the beetles in his mouth so he had a free hand to capture the third. Not a good idea. The beetle reacted by sending out a squirt of horrible, burning juice into his mouth. Darwin spat out the offender and dropped the other beetles.

The experience however didn't put Darwin off beetles. That Christmas he was supposed to visit his girlfriend and her family during the holiday but he didn't arrive. She wrote to him, 'I suppose some dear little Beetles kept you away.' And she was probably right.

Collecting wasn't a new thing for Darwin. As a small boy his pockets were always full of stones, coins, shells and other interesting things he had found. Collecting was quite a fashionable hobby at the time. In grand homes people showed off their stuffed animals and birds, or their exotic plants. But Darwin was not a show-off, or a 'my collection is better than yours' person, even if he was competing with Beetles Babington! He wanted to describe and record the things he found, and he was interested in much more than beetles. At Cambridge Darwin went on long walks with John Henslow, Professor of Botany, and he never stopped asking him questions about plants. Darwin was always wanting things to read which would give him ideas and help him understand. All this made him just the right person to be the naturalist on HMS Beagle and Professor Henslow didn't hesitate to recommend him for the job.

Wherever the Beagle landed Darwin was off collecting. In the Brazilian rainforest he collected 'a number of brilliantly coloured flowers, enough to make a florist go wild.' But collecting was only the first step. Each item had to have a label and be listed. Darwin had to make notes about each one, describing its appearance, where it had been found and any other observations. Without a useful label specimens would be no use to scientists when they arrived back in England after a long sea voyage. Animals had to be preserved or processed, wrapped or bottled, skinned or dried. Plant specimens had to be carefully dried and pressed. It was a lot of work, but Darwin was so busy collecting that his first load of rocks, plants, insects and animals was ready to send back to Professor Henslow just eight months after the Beagle set sail.

Just over a year into the voyage one of the crew, Syms Covington, a 17 year-old who had been a cabin boy and the ship's fiddler, became Darwin's assistant. He worked as a secretary and hunter and also learned to stuff

People Darwin worked with were impressed by his optimistic attitude. Beagle Captain Robert FitzRoy remembered some of Darwin's positive thinking – even when he was seasick! "Well, I am glad we are quietly at sea again, for I shall be able to arrange my collections and set to work more methodically." [2]

animals. Syms and Charles worked so hard and collected so much that the First Lieutenant of the ship complained about the amount of 'rubbish' that was piling up on the deck and the Captain described Darwin and Covington working so earnestly with their pickaxes to extract a huge fossil, which turned out to be the Megatherium. Darwin was very careful about how he kept his notes. He had a Zoological Diary in which he kept observations about plants and animals and a Geological Diary in which he kept notes about rocks and fossils.

Even though he hadn't been a star pupil, Darwin's headmaster from school was really proud of him. Professor Sedgwick once wrote, "He is doing admirably in S. America and has already sent home a collection above all praise. It was the best thing in the world that he went on the Voyage of Discovery." [3]

Covington's main job was helping to keep the Catalogue of Specimens — lists and notes of all the things they had collected. He also packed the barrels so more specimens could be sent to England.

When the specimens arrived in Cambridge they created lots of excitement and interest. Darwin's friends also published extracts from his notes and diaries, so by the time he came back five years later, Darwin was something of a celebrity and treated as a serious scientist. He went on working on the things he had collected on the Beagle.

In some cases, he found that his recordings were not always perfect. On the Galapagos Islands he collected little birds. A scientist in England, John Gould, spotted that they were all finches, although they had different-shaped beaks. Their beak shape depended on whether they ate seeds, cacti or insects. Gould thought that the different types of finch probably came from different islands so they had a different diet depending on their habitat. But he could not be sure as Darwin had not noted exactly where each bird had been found. Darwin immediately began contacting everyone who might have the information they needed about the birds, because this was a very exciting idea and he needed the evidence to prove it.

This kind of work and lots of new experiments that Darwin did to test what he was thinking were all part of his big and challenging idea that all living things must share a common origin.

Challenge questions

- Modern day plant hunters make detailed records, carefully press and dry specimens, do background research and always keep their eyes peeled — just like Darwin.
- Which one of these activities do you think is the most important?
- Which do you think you would be good at?

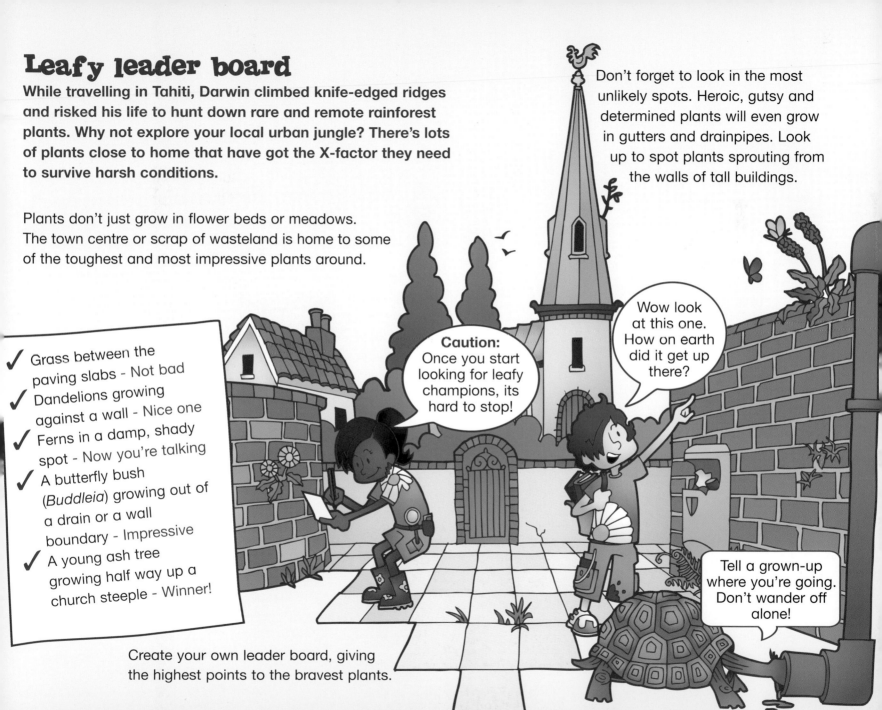

Leafy leader board

While travelling in Tahiti, Darwin climbed knife-edged ridges and risked his life to hunt down rare and remote rainforest plants. Why not explore your local urban jungle? There's lots of plants close to home that have got the X-factor they need to survive harsh conditions.

Plants don't just grow in flower beds or meadows. The town centre or scrap of wasteland is home to some of the toughest and most impressive plants around.

Don't forget to look in the most unlikely spots. Heroic, gutsy and determined plants will even grow in gutters and drainpipes. Look up to spot plants sprouting from the walls of tall buildings.

✓ Grass between the paving slabs - Not bad

✓ Dandelions growing against a wall - Nice one

✓ Ferns in a damp, shady spot - Now you're talking

✓ A butterfly bush (*Buddleia*) growing out of a drain or a wall boundary - Impressive

✓ A young ash tree growing half way up a church steeple - Winner!

Caution: Once you start looking for leafy champions, its hard to stop!

Wow look at this one. How on earth did it get up there?

Tell a grown-up where you're going. Don't wander off alone!

Create your own leader board, giving the highest points to the bravest plants.

Chapter 6: Darwin the Investigator

c.1855, Down House
Darwin aged 46

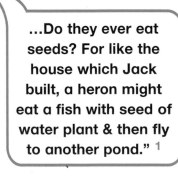

In the same letter as another request, Darwin asked his friend Eyton more questions, looking for even more information about seeds dispersed by animals: "Lastly (if you are not sick of my enquiries) have you ever examined the stomachs of dace and other white fish?...

...Do they ever eat seeds? For like the house which Jack built, a heron might eat a fish with seed of water plant & then fly to another pond." [1]

Charles Darwin buttoned up his warm black coat, pulled on his big black hat, and called the dog. It was time for a thinking walk. He made his way, through the gardens and across the back of Down House to the beginning of the sand-covered path he had made soon after he and his wife, Emma, had moved from London to Kent with their two young children. The path wound through the woods and returned to the house along the side of a hedge-lined field.

At the beginning of the walk was a line of three stones. Darwin knocked aside the first of the stones with his walking stick. He would be moving the second and third as he came round again and again. This was a three stone problem.

Darwin took the Sand Walk at least once every day and often more. Walking helped him to think. Today he was thinking about something he had noticed when he was the naturalist on HMS Beagle more than twenty years before. He was amazed by how seeds got from one place to another — how they dispersed. When he was on the Cocos Islands in the middle of the Indian Ocean he had wondered why it was that he was finding the same plants that grew on the mainland thousands of miles away. How did the plants get there? Could they really have survived a very long journey across the salty sea?

He had been reading the ideas of one scientist who explained the riddle by saying that remote bits of land had originally been joined on to the mainland. But Darwin wasn't happy with this idea. He wanted to understand the whole tricky problem of how seeds got from one place to another. Darwin walked round the Sand Walk until he had decided what to do. He needed to go back to basics and do an experiment.

Back at the house, Darwin sat in his comfortable study and thought some more. His children came in. They slid around on a stool with wheels and drew on bits of paper as they often did when he was working.

Once he had decided what to do, like all experimenters, Darwin had to gather together his equipment first. He collected seeds, made some salty water and even got some sea animals to live in it for a year to check that it was just right. He put the home-made sea water in glass bottles, popped in a variety of seeds, such as lettuce, pepper, cabbage, onion, celery, rhubarb and oats, and waited to see what happened.

Darwin wrote letters every day and asked thousands of new questions, not to mention favours! He was interested in every little detail about how seeds travelled. In one letter, he wrote to his bird expert friend, Eyton, "Do you know when an owl or hawk eats a little bird, how soon it throws up pellet? …How I should like to get a collection of pellets and see whether they contained any seeds capable of germination. Could your gamekeepers find a roosting place and collect a lot for me?" [2]

Darwin watched and carefully noted down the changes in the seeds as they swelled up, changed colour, sunk down to the bottom of the bottles and really started to stink. Sensibly he repeated the experiment using the same types of seeds, but did not put any salt in the water. That was the only way that he could tell if it was the salt or something else that was making a difference to the seeds.

Once the seeds that had been in the salt water were planted Darwin was surprised to find that nearly all of them had survived their salty ordeal and still had the strength to sprout. Some of them, like the celery and rhubarb, began to grow faster than ever.

Darwin was quick to talk things through with his old friend Thomas Hooker. He was a plant expert who had just been appointed Assistant Director of the Royal Botanic Gardens in Kew. They had met first when Darwin returned from the Beagle voyage and showed Hooker some plants from Tierra del Fuego. They had liked each other from the start and now Hooker was a frequent visitor at Down House. At one time in the early days he had been like an assistant, gathering facts Darwin needed. Now he was the kind of trusted friend that Darwin tried out his ideas on. Darwin also shared his findings with the readers of a gardening and farming magazine. He had written to them for advice and felt it was only fair that he should share this new-found information with them.

Darwin wrote thousands of letters to friends and strangers asking for information. He thought lots of different people, gardeners, pigeon breeders, as well as scientists, might be able to help him solve nature's mysteries. He wrote to the islanders in the places he had visited asking them to look out for plants that were not native growing on the shore. He contacted survey vessels like the Beagle and asked them to send him information. He never seemed embarrassed to ask odd or strange questions. He once write to a bird expert asking him to collect some mud from the feet of a wading bird to see if it had any seeds in it. Like all good scientists Darwin knew he would have to find evidence and gather facts to get answers to his questions.

Darwin became so interested in the way that seeds travel that he took his experiments to some rather strange extremes. For thirty days he floated a dead pigeon that had just eaten seeds, in salt water so that he could cut open its body, plant the seeds and watch for signs of sprouting. When some seedlings appeared he realised that when a bird carrying seeds dies and falls into the sea, it's possible that its last meal could end up sprouting on dry land.

Challenge questions

- There are many ways that a seed can spread from its 'parent' plant to the place where it will land, settle and grow. As well as a sea journey, seeds can be transported in the stomach or on the fur of animals, on the wind and sometimes they are 'shot' into the big, wide world by the 'parent' plant. People also play a part in spreading seeds.
- Can you think of how humans might be part of how seeds spread?
- If Darwin was alive today what 21st century method of seed dispersal would he study?

Seedy socks

Charles Darwin went to great lengths to study how seeds are transported from one place to another. He looked at bird droppings to see if they contained seeds.

You'll be pleased to hear that this simple experiment does not involve any poo!

We need:

- An old, large sock
- A large cup full of fresh compost
- A plastic tray or container
- Scissors

Tell a grown-up where you are going. Don't wander off alone

1) Put an old, large sock on over your shoe. You might need to cut the sock a bit to get it on.
2) Walk around a grassy space so the sock picks up seeds and plant material. It's best done in late summer or early autumn.
3) Make small holes in the bottom of the plastic container. Add half the soil.
4) Cut out a small seedy piece of your seedy sock and put it in. Cover it with more soil. Lightly water it and leave it somewhere sunny to sprout.

Hey Lily, wait for me!

I wonder how many seeds I'm collecting

It's amazing – they all look different this close up!

I wonder what will grow

Make an odd sock happy. Find a sock without a pair and you'll bring new meaning to its life

Chapter 7: Darwin the Plant Detective

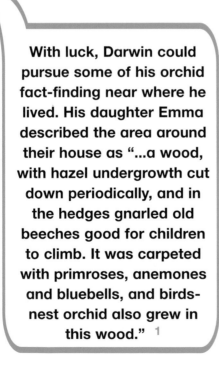

With luck, Darwin could pursue some of his orchid fact-finding near where he lived. His daughter Emma described the area around their house as "...a wood, with hazel undergrowth cut down periodically, and in the hedges gnarled old beeches good for children to climb. It was carpeted with primroses, anemones and bluebells, and birds-nest orchid also grew in this wood." [1]

c.1861, Down House
Darwin aged 52

Charles Darwin, the world-famous plant hunter, tackled some of the greatest scientific mysteries of his time. Like a detective he enjoyed gathering together the necessary evidence to arrive at the truth. Quite often this meant months or years of experimenting, collecting information and recording his thoughts. Even when he had published the book which everyone was arguing about and some were sure had solved one of the biggest mysteries of all, he went on being curious and asking questions. No case was too small or too large. Each one took him closer to understanding the wonders of the natural world.

Darwin did most of his work at home in Down House. Visitors were amazed that this scientist didn't have a laboratory. Instead he used a 'spacious, cheerful room' next to his living room. There he studied just about anything, from worms and seeds to cabbages and pigeons. The garden also served as his outdoor laboratory. He left one part of the lawn untended for three years and his records show that over that time six delicate plant species had gone. In another place he gathered evidence about the ways weed seedlings germinated.

Darwin loved the wild flowers and plants that grew in the fields and hedgerows around his home. A family of flowering plants called orchids really fascinated him. He noticed that the orchids came in all sorts of shapes and sizes. He also noticed that each one had a flower that was perfectly formed to take a visiting bee, moth or fly.

Insects visit flowers for the sweet juicy liquid, or nectar, which they love. Without knowing it, these busy visitors are helping some plants to make seeds. Many of the wonderful orchids which Darwin studied need insects to help make their seeds.

On warmer days, the wild orchids that grew in Darwin's neighbourhood hummed with insects. He watched as they hurried about hunting for sweet nectar. When they found some, the insects uncurled their feeding tubes, which look a bit like tiny rolled-up hosepipes and reached down into the flower to sip their favourite food.

Darwin began to grow orchids in the greenhouses at Down House. He got his children to help him to study the plants, as well as the insects that visited them. Darwin's son once spotted four different moths visiting

the same orchid. His detective work was published in his father's famous book on orchids.

Darwin was as careful with storing his orchid information as he was with all of the other evidence he collected over the years. He kept it in labelled wooden boxes. The boxes held recent newspaper cuttings, notes and half written articles. Note-taking played an important part in Darwin's thinking. He took great care to make notes about all his experiments, even the ones that went wrong. He realised that he might even be able to learn from his embarrassing mistakes.

Of all the 20,000 or so different types of orchid, the one that really got Darwin's detective brain excited was the comet orchid which has a giant white waxy flower.

Darwin loved orchids and shared his growing understanding of the role that insects play in plant life cycles. He told his fellow botanist Mr Bentham, "They are wonderful creatures, these Orchids, and I sometimes think with a glow of pleasure, when I remember making out some little point in their method of fertilisation." [2]

Visitors came to see Darwin from all over the world. A writer visiting from Germany Ernst von Hesse-Wartegg praised Darwin's way of organising his specimens and data. He said, "Darwin has an excellent arrangement, which could be recommended to many another scholar, in the form of a series of wooden boxes." 3

Darwin knew that some of his conclusions might be considered crazy! But he still stuck by them. When his moth idea didn't go down well he said, "This belief of mine has been ridiculed." But he was later proved to be absolutely right. 4

This orchid is usually found on the island of Madagascar, off the east coast of Africa. When Darwin managed to grow comet orchid in his greenhouse, he noticed that the flower had a 25 centimetre-long narrow tube, that held a few drops of sweet nectar. Darwin puzzled over how an insect could possibly reach down to the bottom of the tube to take a sip of the nectar. The tube was just too narrow for insects to squeeze through. If there wasn't an insect that could reach that far down the tube then why was nectar found there? Moths have long feeding tubes that they use to suck up nectar, a bit like a drinking straw. So, could there be a moth flying around the Madagascan forests with a massive 25 centimetre-long feeding tube? Darwin thought so. Insect experts thought he was crazy. Who can blame them? No one had seen a moth like that, so where was the proof?

Many years after Darwin died, naturalists discovered a moth in Madagascar with a wingspan of 15 centimetres and a feeding tube that measures 25 centimetres — just perfect for sipping nectar from the comet orchid. The case of the mysterious orchid was finally closed.

Challenge questions

- A real-life detective has to ask questions, be on the lookout at all times and make notes before they can solve a crime. A detective might also take a guess and then try to prove that they're right.
- Which of these detective skills do you think is most important to a scientist and why?

Spud break-out

Darwin was fascinated by how plants grow. He grew lots of plants to test how different conditions - like the amount of light - affect their growth. Now it's your turn to try growing something!

1) Make a potato 'prison'! First cut a hole in one of the short ends of the shoe box.
2) Balance the potato on the open end of the yoghurt pot. Put it in the shoe box at the opposite end.
3) Cut two pieces of cardboard as wide as the shoe box. These should stand up like walls. Cut a hole in each one and slot them into the box.
4) Put the lid on the so the potato only gets light through the hole in the short end of the box.
5) Put the box in a sunny spot. Peek in to see what happens over a few weeks!

Look, make it a bit like this

Paint a face on the box so the sprouts grow out of an eye or mouth. Check with your friends to see how well their spuds are doing too! Did they grow them in a sunny spot? What difference does that make?

Chapter 8: Darwin's big ideas

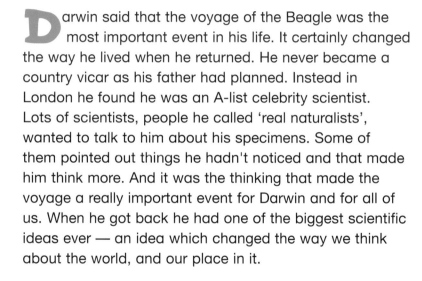

Thinking problems through well was part of Darwin's way of working. Sometimes it took him a while to work out what the problem actually was. "I suppose that I am a very slow thinker, for you would be surprised at the number of years it took me to see clearly what some of the problems were which had to be solved." [1]

Darwin said that the voyage of the Beagle was the most important event in his life. It certainly changed the way he lived when he returned. He never became a country vicar as his father had planned. Instead in London he found he was an A-list celebrity scientist. Lots of scientists, people he called 'real naturalists', wanted to talk to him about his specimens. Some of them pointed out things he hadn't noticed and that made him think more. And it was the thinking that made the voyage a really important event for Darwin and for all of us. When he got back he had one of the biggest scientific ideas ever — an idea which changed the way we think about the world, and our place in it.

Darwin thought long and hard about the meaning of all the things he had seen and found during the voyage. At Down House he walked his 'thinking path' every day and filled many notebooks. Gradually Darwin got an idea. It wasn't like a flash of lightning but it was exciting and a bit frightening. Darwin began to believe that the plants and creatures he had collected hadn't always been like that. At one time, millions of years ago they had all been the same and gradually, very, very slowly, they changed how they were. We call this idea 'evolution'.

But Darwin couldn't understand why all living things change. Then he read what Thomas Malthus was thinking. Malthus's idea was that when there is a famine or an epidemic, the weakest people die. That harsh fact gave Darwin more ideas about plants and animals and why they change. The plants and animals that have the most successful adaptations survive the hardships that nature throws at them. Nature, he thought, seemed to 'select' features that helped with survival — cunning camouflage, a prickly leaf, a bird's beak that could crack seeds to find food. This part of his big idea he called 'natural selection'.

It was a really big idea. Most people at that time believed the earth was only about 60,000 years old and that each plant and animal was created by God, and did not change. Darwin thought his idea might be too big and worried about how people would react. For twenty years he didn't tell the world about it. He went on thinking and filled many notebooks with his ideas. He did lots more experiments, some lasting years, to test his ideas. Like most scientists he needed to discuss his work with others and get their feedback. There was no texting, MSN or emails, he just wrote hundreds of letters. He shared his theories about evolution and natural selection only with his closest friends.

Then one day something arrived in the post that made Darwin think again. It was an essay from Alfred Russel Wallace, a young traveller and collector. He had come up with exactly the same theory that Darwin had been silent about for so long. Wallace wasn't worried about what people would think and was ready to tell everyone. Would they fight about who had the 'evolution' idea first? Luckily they didn't. Instead their friends arranged for their theories to be presented together at a world-famous natural history society in London. A year later in 1859 Charles Darwin put his ideas into a book called *On the Origin of Species* — one of the most important books ever.

Darwin's theories did upset lots of people. They wouldn't accept them — some people still don't.

Darwin the Conservationist
The voyage of the Beagle was important to Darwin in another way too.

It made him see the world in a different way and turned him into one of the world's first conservationists — someone keen to protect the natural world from being destroyed.

As a young man, like many others at the time, who had spare time and money, Darwin loved to collect eggs and go shooting, hunting birds, rabbits, rats and other mammals. In the early stages of the Beagle voyage, while travelling and collecting, Darwin used his rifle enthusiastically. But gradually he used it less and less.

He discovered that he preferred 'the pleasure of observing and reasoning'. He wanted to try to understand the wildlife around him without hunting.

On his travels Darwin ate tortoise meat though he thought it tasted best in a soup. Later, when he found out that the tortoises on one of the islands of Mauritius were becoming very rare he signed an important letter sent to the governor of the island. The letter asked the governor to do something about this problem.

After his travels and a lifetime of studying plants, fossils, the weather and even worms, it became clearer than ever to Darwin that all living things are connected and need to be treasured and cared for. Darwin wrote to Britain's biggest gardening organisation, The Royal Horticultural Society, asking them to stop giving prizes to plant collectors who dug up rare plants just to win competitions. Darwin was worried that some of those plants would be lost forever. The more he found out about plants, the more Darwin learned to value them.

Many plant scientists today feel the same way today. At the Royal Botanic Gardens in Kew, London, scientists dry, press and label parts of plants, just as Darwin did, so that they can be stored in a special collection called a 'herbarium' and studied. So far they have about seven million pressed plants at Kew. The oldest pressed plant specimen was gathered from the wild over 250 years ago. There are also hundreds of pressed plant specimens

that were collected by Darwin and given to Kew. Each year plant hunters working in different parts of the world continue to send back new plants that have been discovered to add to the collection. They are continuing the work that Darwin and others before him started over 200 years ago.

One way to protect a plant for future generations is to store its seed in a seed bank, like Kew's Millennium Seed Bank. Unlike plants, seeds can be kept for many years and can then be grown if they are needed. Experts at the Millennium Seed Bank are collecting, recording and storing seeds from the world's rarest and most at-risk plants. This work will help us to save some of the thousands of plants that may disappear forever.

If Darwin was alive now, he would probably be amazed and delighted to see how his work is being continued by today's plant hunters.

Challenge questions

- When do you do your best thinking.....?
- So what puts plants in danger? Why do you think we might need seed banks in the future?

Outdoor art

Darwin was often amazed at the beauty and variety of objects that he collected on his walks and expeditions.

Why not celebrate your surroundings by making a work of art outdoors. The good news is that you don't need to be good at art to create a natural masterpiece.

Artist Andy Goldsworthy uses leaves, ice and stone in his artwork. His sculptures melt or fade but that's OK. He does that on purpose. It reminds him (and me) how fragile our natural world is.

Hmm, leaves or bark for this bit? I'm going to take a photo of it every day to see how it changes.

These leaves are different colours, but they came from one tree. I'll make a 'leaf clock'. It shows plants change over time.

1) Take a walk outside in your local garden, park, field or forest. Collect whatever catches your eye – fallen leaves, blossom, stones, twigs and seeds. **Remember:** Avoid stuff that's growing or belongs to someone.

2) Don't take the collection back home. Create your art here and now.

3) Once finished, don't move your art, leave it to sit and be! The sun might fade it or the wind could blow it away.

REFERENCES

Chapter 1
1) From *The life and letters of Charles Darwin*, by his son Francis Darwin in 1887.
2) Charles Darwin, writing in 1838.
3) From *The life and letters of Charles Darwin*, by his son Francis Darwin in 1887.
4) From *The life-work of Lord Avebury (Sir John Lubbock) 1834-1913* by Ursula Grant Duff, ed. 1924.

Chapter 2
1) From *The life and letters of Charles Darwin*, by his son Francis Darwin in 1887.
2) From *The life and letters of Charles Darwin*, by his son Francis Darwin in 1887.
3) From a letter to his sister written in April 1831.
4) From *The life and letters of Charles Darwin*, by his son Francis Darwin in 1887.

Chapter 3
1) From *The life and letters of Charles Darwin*, by his son Francis Darwin, 1887.
2) Entry in Darwin's *Beagle Diary* from 1 March 1832, on visiting Bahia.
3) From Darwin's book *The Voyage of the Beagle*, 1839.

Chapter 4
1) Entry in Darwin's *Beagle Diary* from January 1832, in St Jago.
2) Entry in Darwin's *Beagle Diary* from April 1832.
3) Entry in Darwin's *Beagle Diary* – 29th Feb, 1832.
4) Entry in Darwin's *Beagle Diary* from March 1832.

Chapter 5
1) From *The autobiography of Charles Darwin 1809-1882*.
2) Darwin's words on leaving Porto Praya in March 1832, according to Beagle Captain Robert FitzRoy in a letter to the Admiralty. Darwin Correspondence Project, www.darwinproject.ac.uk
3) Darwin Correspondence Project, www.darwinproject.ac.uk

Chapter 6
1) Darwin writing to his bird expert friend T. C. Eyton in August 1856 Darwin Correspondence Project, www.darwinproject.ac.uk
2) Darwin writing to his bird expert friend T. C. Eyton in August 1856 Darwin Correspondence Project, www.darwinproject.ac.uk

Chapter 7
1) A description, by Darwin's daughter, of a piece woodland near their home.
From *A Century of Family Letters*, by Emma Darwin, June 1887.
2) In a letter from Charles Darwin to a fellow botanist, Mr Bentham, from *The life and letters of Charles Darwin*, by his son Francis Darwin in 1887.
3) From *Bei Charles Darwin* [At Charles Darwin's] a newspaper article by Ernst von Hesse-Wartegg, 1880.
4) From *The various contrivances by which orchids are fertilised by insects* by Charles Darwin, 1877.

Chapter 8
1) From *The autobiography of Charles Darwin 1809-1882*.

© The Board of Trustees of the Royal Botanic Gardens, Kew 2009
First published in 2009 by Royal Botanic Gardens, Kew, Richmond, Surrey, TW9 3AB, UK

ISBN 978-1-84246-420-5

British Library Cataloguing in Publication Data
A catalogue record for this book is available from the British Library

All the materials in this book are downloadable free of charge from The Great Plant Hunt website www.kew.org/greatplanthunt

Printed in Spain by Imago

Mixed Sources
Product group from well-managed forests, and other controlled sources
www.fsc.org Cert no.TT-COC-002563
© 1996 Forest Stewardship Council
FSC

For RBG Kew:
Executive Producer
Angela McFarlane
Authors
Aileen O'Riordan, Pat Triggs
Illustrations
Jamie Lenman: Lily, Ash and Joseph characters
Guy Allen: Activity illustrations
Sophie Allsopp: Figure of Charles Darwin
Palm House image © The Board of Trustees of the Royal Botanic Gardens, Kew 2009
Print Design & Prepress (The Templar Company Ltd), Jonathan Lambert, Caroline Reeves, Rachel Ellen Parker

Contributors
Gail Bromley MBE, Susan Allan, Sarah Bell
Project Manager, Senior Producer
Khairoun Abji
Research
Megan Gimber

For The Wellcome Trust:
Clare Matterson: Director of Medicine, Society and History
Daniel Glaser: Development Manager in Public Engagement
Amy Sanders: Project Manager, Darwin 200